I0423500

Willpower And Self Control

Strengthen Your Willpower Today With Mind Performance Hacks To Achieve Your Full Potential

Table of Contents

Introduction

I want to thank you and congratulate you for purchasing the book *Willpower And Self Control.*

This book contains proven steps and strategies on how to successfully boost your self-control and willpower.

This book also contains information regarding the importance of self-control and willpower. Here, you will learn how to improve your life by increasing your levels of self-control and willpower.

Thanks again for purchasing this book. I hope you enjoy it!

Chapter 1: What Is Self-Control and Willpower?

Self-control and willpower are the pillars of your inner strength. This strength can be stored and used whenever necessary, much like a battery. When the battery of your inner strength is fully charged, you can use its power for a variety of purposes. Conversely, when you charge the battery of your inner strength on a regular basis, you can use its power at your disposal each time you need it.

What is willpower? Willpower is basically a form of inner strength expressed as the determination to act on and carry out decisions and plans, despite discomfort, laziness, external obstacles, and internal resistance. Willpower includes the concepts of assertiveness, inner power, and decisiveness. It is actually the inner power that allows you to ignore temptations, disturbances, and distractions, which may prevent you from fulfilling your duties and achieving your goals. Also, willpower provides you with the confidence and strength you need to agree and disagree with others and to express opinions without giving in to pressure or being swayed by the opinions of others.

How do you know when you have exerted willpower? For example, you have decided you want to go for a run, but you found out your favorite television show is also about to start. What do you do? Do you still go out and run, or do you stay at home and watch the show? If you chose to stick to your initial decision to run, then you have successfully exerted willpower. Another example in which you can demonstrate willpower is when you are trying to follow a weight loss program and refuse to indulge in sweets, pastries, and fatty foods at a party. You will also prove that you have self-control if you do not give in to your friends' insistence to try out foods that are not allowed in your diet.

Also, if someone told you a secret, you are supposed to keep that secret. If you can resist the urge of spilling it to your spouse, sibling, or friend, then you have successfully demonstrated your willpower. You can also say that you have strong willpower if you face difficulties without giving up.

With strong willpower, you will have what it takes to face, deal with, and solve your problems. Keep in mind that strong willpower should not be confused with aggression. Willpower is a skill that can be developed and strengthened with regular practice and exercise. Aggression, on the other hand, is a behavior that uses excessive force and does not consider the rights of other people.

How about self-control? Self-control works hand-in-hand with willpower. It involves self-discipline, patience, and ability to control impulsive behavior. Self-control gives you endurance, perseverance and restraint. It also enables you to deal with hardships, obstacles and inconveniences.

What are examples of situations that display self-control? You have self-control if you can fight temptations and fulfill your obligations without delay. You have good self-control if you are not easily persuaded or distracted by other people, things or events. You also have good self-control if you can attend to your priorities and obligations instead of losing your focus to unnecessary tasks.

With self-control, you can avoid anything excessive. Keep in mind that too much of anything is not healthy. Hence, you should always practice self-control when it comes to eating, working or engaging in pleasurable activities. You should employ moderation to everything you do. Self-control is synonymous with self-discipline, which is also a form of inner strength and is necessary for efficiently pursuing goals and dealing with daily issues.

Chapter 2: The Importance of Self-Control and Willpower

Self-control and willpower are crucial to managing your life properly. Without self-control, you put yourself at risk of life-threatening, long-term consequences. If you do not practice self-control, then you are no different from any other animal. As a human, you have the extraordinary ability to control your own thoughts and behaviors without relying on instinct and aggression.

Each person must discipline himself, so he can live a happier and more structured life. He needs to practice self-control, in order to resist temptations that produce negative consequences. If he gives in to his desires and indulgences, he will lose control over different aspects of his life. If everyone did this, society as we know it would fall apart. Hence, keep in mind that self-control is a vital aspect of social- and self-development.

With self-control, you will increase your patience. You can restrain your actions and increase your tolerance or staying power. When you exercise self-control, you increase your self-esteem and other people view you as someone with discipline and control over his actions and emotions. Nonetheless, it is actually easier to be directed and controlled by others than to exercise self-control, because exercising self-control requires tremendous determination and grit.

If you lack self-control, you may be susceptible to criminal tendencies, aggressive behavior, and self-neglect. You can be detrimental not only to yourself but also to others close to you and to society. In addition, your lack of self-control can have serious repercussions such as drained emotions and reclusive tendencies. This is why you need to strike a balance between all aspects of your life and learn how to use self-control appropriately.

Chapter 3: How Much Self-Control Do You Have and How Can You Develop Willpower?

In the book *Willpower*, authors John Teirney and Roy Baumeister talk about the seminal marshmallow research study done by Walter Mischel. According to this study, a group of 4 year old children were given a marshmallow each and told not to eat it until fifteen minutes had passed. If they did not eat their marshmallows, they would be given another one.

However, some kids could not wait for fifteen minutes, so they ate their marshmallows right away. Others waited awhile before giving in and eating theirs. Only a few children waited patiently until fifteen minutes had passed, and these children received another marshmallow as a prize. The study does not end here, though. These children were monitored as they grew up.

They attended the same school, and those who ate their marshmallows right away were more prone to getting into trouble. Children with lower self-control were found to have lower grades, lower SAT scores, poorer health, lower salaries, and a greater chance of being imprisoned. Researchers concluded that the trait of self-control can predict success in education and life in general.

Self-control is very important to achieving success. It basically makes or breaks your chances of succeeding in life. So, how much of it do you actually have? Many of you probably play computer games or watch television on a regular basis. If you were told to do something less enjoyable in exchange of more hours to play computer games or watch television, would you do it?

If you were given a chance to watch television or play computer games for one hour today but have one more hour the next day provided that you do not watch television or play computer games today, would you rather enjoy yourself now or wait until tomorrow? How well do you think you would do at depriving yourself of today's pleasure with the guarantee that you can have more pleasure tomorrow?

You need to be honest with yourself and evaluate your recent experiences. Do you engage in programs or courses to improve your skills? Do you prevent yourself from becoming an impulsive buyer or shopaholic? Do you eat well, sleep enough and exercise regularly? Have you committed illegal or shameful acts without considering their possible consequences?

Rate yourself from one to ten with ten being meaning you can effectively control yourself to achieve better results. Rate yourself with a zero if you think that you are not disciplined enough to reach your goals. Remember that the first step toward greater personal control is recognizing how valuable it is. The second step is acknowledging that you need to develop more of it.

Once you recognize how important willpower is, you should want and start to develop it. Think of what you can do today to successfully develop it. You should also practice exerting your willpower until you get used to it. According to research, controlling even small patterns of your behavior can increase your self-control and improve your overall willpower.

For instance, you can decide to exercise for at least ten minutes every morning upon waking up or drink a glass of water before you eat breakfast. These healthy habits can actually improve your willpower, so when you try to do other tasks, you will realize that your willpower has become stronger. Choose to take on small new activities to improve your life and mold you into a self-directed individual.

To start, you can find a benchmark in your past. This can be an experience in which you exerted self-control in order to obtain a vital result. For instance, you recall working and going to school at the same time. Both work and studies require a lot of effort and perseverance. If you managed to do both, then you have practiced self-control and willpower, and this can be your benchmark.

Think about this experience and remember your feelings and efforts during this time. Recall the moment when you finally accomplished your goals. You can also recall other situations that enabled you to display self-control and willpower. Also recognize that willpower is crucial yet limited, meaning you can be full of it in the morning and slowly lose it as the day goes by.

Hence, you must use your willpower wisely. Also, see to it that you maintain a healthy lifestyle by eating well, drinking plenty of water, getting sufficient rest, and avoiding bad vices, such as smoking, drinking alcoholic beverages, and using illegal drugs. Additionally, you need to take the offensive. Tierney and Baumeister both urge people to take the initiative to become determined in developing willpower.

For instance, you can develop project plans, cultivate values, think positively, and move forward with your life. You can also support your thoughts with religious beliefs if you feel that that would make them more effective. Start setting goals that are worthwhile yet achievable. In order to avoid diluting your powers, keep your goals few. Remember that focus is also very important for you stay productive.

After formulating your goals, you must start right away. Do not procrastinate because it can immobilize you. You have to fight procrastination with serious determination, and one way you can fight it is through pre-commitment. For instance, leave your credit card at home, so you will not be tempted to buy unnecessary things when you go to the mall. You can also write down your commitments to remind yourself of them.

Your next step in the offensive for achieving success is to keep track. For instance, if you plan to avoid eating dessert, keep a daily record. You can also mark it on your calendar. If you follow this practice, you will not only be able to record your success, but you will also reinforce it. When you achieve your goals, do not forget to reward yourself. Give yourself a treat to keep you motivated.

Furthermore, keep in mind that determination is what willpower thrives on, what drives you to suck it up and keep moving forward until you reach the finish line. With determination, you will stay driven in reaching your goals.

Chapter 4: Exercises That Enhance Self-Control and Willpower

Now that you have learned about self-control and willpower, it is time to learn how to strengthen them. As you have already read, self-control and willpower can be strengthened with practice and exercise. Nonetheless, you can also strengthen them through meditation and relaxation. In this chapter, you will find out how exercise can help you improve your self-control and willpower.

If you manage to go to the gym every morning instead of opting to keep sleeping, then you have good self-control. However, this is not enough. Being able to hit the gym instead of sleeping in is not sufficient to prove that you are a determined individual. Fortunately, exercising can help increase your self-control and willpower. In fact, researchers have already found evidence linking exercise to self-control.

Researchers from the Netherlands, for instance, have found that exercise can help improve brain functions, including self-control. They have also found that exercise can help you improve your memory and become mentally flexible. A review published in the British Journal of Sports Medicine showed that exercise can have great benefits on the brains of young adults, children and adolescents.

The researchers broke down their results according to the type of exercise, such as ten-minute and forty-minute sessions as well as long programs that have multiple weekly sessions. Overall, it was found that single exercise sessions can give a moderate boost to the brain functions of all age groups. Aside from young adults, children, and adolescents, these exercise sessions can help increase the self-control of individuals aged 18 to 35 years.

The researchers believe that exercise helps boost self-control by increasing the flow of oxygen and blood to the prefrontal cortex, the area of the brain that controls higher brain functions. Other studies have also highlighted the link between brainpower and exercise, including how it can help you improve your creativity and deal with monetary cravings.

Keep in mind that just like your muscles, your self-control can vary in strength. You should take note that even well developed muscles can feel like jelly sometimes, especially when they have experienced too much strain. Likewise, your self-control can deteriorate if you do not maintain it properly. If you focus too much on hassles, stressors and distractions, your willpower and self-control will weaken.

Then again, depletion is not permanent. Once you rest and take a break, you can gain back your strength. If you want to have more self-control, you can also get more. However, if you do gain more self-control, you have to exercise it more. You have already read examples of practicing self-control from a previous chapter. If you make practicing self-control a habit, you will be able to strengthen it.

In a study conducted by psychologist Mark Murayen, a group of adult women and men were asked to either use a handgrip or avoid sweets for a couple of weeks. The group that chose to avoid sweets was asked to avoid eating candy, cookies, cake, and desserts as much as possible. On the other hand, the group that chose to use a handgrip was asked to hold their handgrips twice a day for as long as they can.

Both of these tasks require participants to practice self-control. One group was required to resist temptation while the other one was required to overcome physical discomfort. At the end of two weeks, Murayen found that the participants of the study had improved in completing a challenging computerized concentration task that required a lot of self-control.

Both groups, regardless of what kind of self-control exercise they had, were able to significantly improve their willpower and strengthen their self-control in just a couple of weeks. In another study, psychologists Ken Cheng and Megan Oaten gave participants free gym memberships and customized exercise programs designed by professional trainers.

These exercise programs included free-weights, resistance training, and aerobics. After exercising on a regular basis for a couple of months, the participants were able to increase their ability to perform various laboratory self-control tasks. Also, they were able to improve many other aspects of their life. These men and women were able to reduce their smoking, drinking, and indulgence in junk food.

They were also able to control their tempers and manage their finances better. They no longer leave used dishes in the sink or put important tasks off until later. They also no longer miss appointments or receive poor grades. In fact, the aspects of their lives that involved self-control dramatically improved. This only proves that exercise does not only improve muscles, but it also improves self-control.

The studies with regard to self-control have used different approaches, from brushing teeth to directing people, to refraining from saying bad words to using the non-dominant hand to do things. Just sitting in an upright position can already help you boost your self-control. These methods may have been different, but all of them force you to do something that you would rather not do and that trains you to fight against your urge to give up, give in, or lose interest.

Exercises That Improve Your Self-Control and Willpower

Do Things that You Enjoy

If you have always wanted to see a movie or a play but are too busy to go to the cinema or theater, now is the time for you to do it. If you have always wanted to go to the beach or try out a new restaurant but always put it off, you should go now. Likewise, if you have always wanted to eat a particular dish, you should definitely clear your schedule so you can cook it.

Usually, people put off doing the things they really want to do because they feel there are other, more important things they have to take care of. For instance, if you want to travel but you do not want to miss work, you are focusing on the more pressing task. So what should you do? You should take a vacation and do the things you really enjoy.

You should do things you like even if it means sacrificing other things that are important to you. Once you have decided to pursue the thing you really like, you should make a schedule. Set a date and time for this activity, and make sure you drop all your other engagements and make this activity a priority.

You may feel lazy or tempted to procrastinate. Do not give in to temptation and stick with your decision. Execute the activity as you planned, and do not allow anything in the way of your success.

Practicing this exercise lets you combine experiencing pleasure and obtaining inner strength. If you practice it often, you will learn to enjoy your life while also strengthening your self-control and willpower. Additionally, you will strengthen your determination and decisiveness.

Turn Off the Music

When you listen to your favorite song or music, you should try to turn it off for several minutes. You may feel reluctant to this, but doing so can actually improve your self-discipline and decision-making skills. Once you turn the music off, you will prove that you are capable of overcoming inner resistance. Yes, you will miss the music, but you will gain inner strength, which is more important.

You should do this exercise for a week. Turn off the radio whenever your favorite song plays. This exercise will help you overcome your inner resistance and strengthen your self-discipline and willpower.

Wash the Dishes

All throughout the day, whenever you see a dirty plate, glass, cup or utensil, you should wash it by hand. Do not place it inside your dishwasher or ask someone else to wash it for you. This can be quite an inconvenience. However, doing this exercise can train your self-discipline and willpower. It also helps you overcome laziness and inner resistance. You should do this exercise for several days, until you no longer feel that washing the dishes is such an inconvenience.

Hold a Glass with the Opposite Hand

If you are used to holding your glass with your right hand, try holding it with your left hand. Likewise, if you are used to holding your glass with your left hand, try holding it with your right hand. At first, you may find it difficult and uncomfortable to hold your glass with your opposite hand.

However, you will increase your inner strength if you ignore your discomfort and continue to use your weaker hand. This exercise will train you to overcome inner resistance and act in spite of discomfort. If you are able to execute a simple act, you will be able to do more significant acts in the long run.

Do this exercise for several days until you no longer find it uncomfortable or inconvenient to hold the glass with your other hand.

Peel a Fruit

To do this exercise, you need a fruit with a peel, such as an orange or an apple, and a knife. Sit down on a comfortable chair and slowly peel the fruit. You can start peeling it from the upper side, around it, and all the way to the bottom. Try to remove the peel in one piece.

After this exercise, you should be able to get the peel off the fruit without breaking it. The act of patiently and slowly peeling the fruit is what truly matters, so it is alright if you break the peel. This exercise will develop your patience, self-discipline and attention.

Chapter 5: Using Meditation to Improve Self-Control and Willpower

Aside from physical exercise, you can also improve your self-control and willpower through meditation.

Meditation and Willpower

Deborah Kotz, a journalist, published an article in the United States World News and Report about the strategies to improve willpower and how mindfulness can strengthen self-control. According to the article, practicing mindfulness meditation for several minutes everyday can improve willpower by building up gray matter in the parts of the brain that control the decision-making process and regulate emotions.

If you pay attention to the things that happen around you, in your mind, and in your body, you will find it easier to tune in to your choices and control them. Thus, if you want to boost your willpower, practice meditation techniques to help you improve your focus, self-compassion, mindfulness and strength to deal with cravings and stress.

Guided Meditation Practices

Guided meditation practices are specially created to support your ability to make decisions and handle cravings and stress. These practices also shift your body and brain into a state that lets you acquire more strength, energy, and focus, so you can overcome difficult challenges and temptations instead of giving into them or giving up. There are various styles out there, which are available as MP3s you can use to guide you. You should choose the style that works best for you.

You can try the fifteen-minute Guided Concentration Meditation Practice, which is a concentration practice that helps focus and stabilize your mind. You can complete this practice in five, ten, or fifteen minutes. Once you finish, you should acknowledge your success of sitting, no matter how distracted or focused you were. As you continue to practice this, you will train your brain to make conscious choices and focus your attention.

You can also try the Breath Focus Meditation with Mindfulness of Breath and Body, which starts with breath focus and shifts into mindfulness of breath, body, thoughts, emotions and sensations. Do not forget to use labels in identifying perceptions and sensations. Once you label these, notice how they smell, feel, and sound, and then come back to your breathing. This practice will help you become more aware of the choices you make and how your behavior is triggered by your thoughts, emotions and environment.

Another great practice you can try is Guided Meditation on Inner Calm. It runs for ten minutes and makes use of the principle of desensitization. This principle is frequently used to deal with phobias, addictions, stress, trauma and conflict. With this practice, you will be asked to enter a state of relaxation and recall situations that cause you stress. Then, you will be asked to go back into your state of relaxation. Note that if this practice makes you feel uncomfortable instead of relaxed, you should stop.

Guided Relaxation is also ideal for when you have ten minutes to spare. It involves visualization and breath awareness. This practice is recommended for use every day if you want to reduce your levels of stress. It also prompts a reduction in automatic behaviors, from smoking to overspending and other addictions.

You can also try Loving Kindness and Compassion for Yourself. It is a fifteen-minute meditation practice designed to help you develop compassion for yourself. According to research, compassion for oneself is crucial for dealing with stress and setbacks in life. It is especially important if you want to make a significant change in your life, such as losing weight or quitting a bad vice. With this practice, you will be asked to recall memories, feelings, and thoughts of love, tenderness, empathy, affection and concern for yourself.

Furthermore, you can try Guided Yoga Nidra Meditation. This meditation practice lasts for thirty minutes and it will take you through the processes of welcoming awareness, breath sensing, body sensing, inner resource, mindfulness and heartfelt intention. Compared to the other practices, this one is fairly long at thirty minutes. Nonetheless, it is highly recommended that you do all of it instead of skipping ahead or stopping. You should do this meditation practice when you are not busy so you have enough time to complete it.

Take note that you might fall asleep while meditating. In case you do fall asleep, do not beat yourself up, because falling asleep is acceptable when you have only just started to meditate. Over time, you become accustomed to meditating and you will find it easier to remain awake. Meditation can help you shift your mind and body, reduce stress, grasp your core values, and reach your goals. It will also enable you to make conscious choices in your everyday life.

Meditation and Self-Control

Not everyone has the same level of self-control. Some people have a good sense of it, while others completely lack it. Fortunately, self-control is something that is not permanently set. This means that you can improve your self-control and have a better life. With meditation, improving your self-control is possible.

Meditation teaches you how to stay clear-headed in the heat of the moment. People tend to like instant gratification and want to immediately feel better no matter what the ramifications are. In the heat of the moment, your long-term goals can seem vague and distant, and you might forget about the guilt and regret you will feel after you get your fix, whether you smoke a cigarette or eat junk food.

However, when you learn your inner thought patterns during meditation, you immediately notice the difference between needing and wanting. Meditation helps you realize the shame and guilt you may feel if you cheat on your diet. It will enable you to reach your long-term goals more easily.

Meditation also activates the willpower part of your brain. According to a study at the Duke University-Caltech in 2009, individuals with high levels of willpower activate their dorsolateral prefrontal cortex, a part of the brain that is also active during meditation.

In addition, meditation releases brain chemicals that make you feel good; thus, replacing your cravings. Endorphins and dopamine get released in your brain whenever you get your unhealthy fix. Such brain chemicals function to soothe the stress response in your body, so whenever you smoke a cigarette or eat junk food, you automatically feel good. These instant fixes feel good initially but will have negative consequences for your health.

If you practice meditation, you will be able to achieve the same "feel good" feeling but without the negative consequences. In fact, meditation can even improve your health in a natural way. If you practice meditation on a regular basis, you can reduce your cravings and urges. You can also reduce stress, clear your mind, and increase your willpower.

Meditation can significantly reduce your anxiety and stress levels that cause you to have unhealthy cravings and urges in the first place. As you know, stress can lead to numerous health problems, such as stroke and heart diseases. According to researchers, meditation is actually more beneficial than physical exercise when it comes to reducing anxiety and stress levels.

Three-Step Meditation Technique

If you wish to boost your willpower, this three-step meditation technique will help you achieve your goal. It is simple and easy to do. More importantly, it will get your blood rushing to your prefrontal cortex and make the most of your brainpower.

1. Remain seated for a while. You can choose to sit on a chair or on the ground. If you sit on a chair, see to it that you keep your feet flat on the floor. If you sit on the ground, you should cross your legs. Whichever position you choose, make sure that you resist the urge to move. As much as possible, you should ignore itches. Do not fidget in your seat or change positions. It is important for you to sit still, so you can learn to not automatically follow your impulses.

2. Focus on your breathing. You should keep your eyes closed and turn your attention to the way you breathe in and breathe out. Say "inhale" to yourself when you breathe in, and say "exhale" when you breathe out. If you notice your mind wandering off, bring it back immediately and focus on your breathing once more. This technique will activate your prefrontal cortex and quiet the craving and stress centers of your brain.

3. Notice how your mind wanders and how you breathe. After several minutes, you should stop saying "inhale" and "exhale" to yourself. Instead, you should solely focus on your breathing sensation. You may notice your mind wandering off for some time, but if you start to think of something else you should turn your attention back to your breathing. If you find it difficult to focus and keep your mind from

wandering, you can say "inhale" and "exhale" again for a few more rounds. This technique will help improve your self-control and self-awareness.

Chapter 6: Using Yoga to Improve Self-Control and Willpower

Practicing yoga can improve your self-control, your willpower, and your ability to overcome bad habits. You can also enhance your self-discipline when you practice with control and precision whenever you train on your mat. Through yoga, you can improve your thinking, outlook and attitude. According to studies, being kind to yourself can also improve your willpower.

Kelly McGonigal, a lecturer and health psychologist at Stanford University and author of the book The Willpower Instinct, states that willpower is not rigid self-control but rather your ability to do things that matter to you even when it is difficult. She also says you can strengthen your resolve if you cultivate mindfulness through yoga and other similar practices.

Yoga allows you to improve your willpower by doing challenging poses, finding your breath, and focusing on the sensations within your body. When you do these, you feel uncomfortable yet you also learn how to stay put. Likewise, whenever you are faced with a temptation or craving you would prefer to pass up, you experience discomfort.

When this happens, you should pause and breathe into it. Tune in to your body and give yourself some space to come up with a decision using your willpower response instead of your stress response. McGonigal agrees that taking a brief moment to reflect can greatly help you avoid falling back into old patterns. Yoga allows you to remember what you want and have the willingness and energy to achieve it.

If you just started yoga, however, there is no need for you to exert too much effort. You can simply lie on your back and put your legs up against a wall. Then, breathe through your belly for five to fifteen minutes. In order to build willpower, you should push through discomfort. Do the yoga poses with fifteen to thirty seconds more than what feels comfortable for you.

You can also enroll in a Bikram or restorative yoga class. Choose a yoga type that best suits your needs. Yoga can help you deal with daily stress and develop willpower. McGonigal states that the most ideal way to develop willpower is by resting, stopping for a while, and resetting yourself so you may pursue the things that matter most to you.

Chapter 7: Improve Your Self-Control and Willpower with a Good Diet

According to a study done at Texas University, self-control is a limited resource that can be strengthened by certain foods. Roy Baumeister, a psychology professor at Florida State University, found that blood glucose levels and self-control are related.

In a study, participants were made to watch a video. Some of them were instructed not to show any facial emotions, while others were not given instructions. After watching the video, the blood glucose levels of those who exerted self-control in showing their emotions had dropped. On the other hand, those who reacted freely while watching the video managed to retain their blood glucose levels.

Later on, the participants were given a concentration test that required them to identify the colors of the words displayed. Those who did not show any reactions while watching the video were found to have the lowest test scores. This suggests that the self-control of these people has been depleted by the video challenge.

Nonetheless, researchers have also found that restoring blood glucose levels can replenish self-control. In one study, participants who drank sugar-sweetened lemonade and raised their glucose levels were able to perform better on self-control tests compared to those who had artificially-sweetened drinks that did not affect their glucose levels. Due to these findings, it has been proven that glucose indeed affects many functions of the brain.

In order for you to maintain your glucose levels, you should eat protein for breakfast. You can have fish, eggs, oats or porridge. You should also reduce your consumption of carbs and wheat, but increase your consumption of whole wheat bread, brown rice, and rye. Never skip breakfast because this can lead to poor brain function, distractibility, and bad mood.

A breakfast that is high in protein will elevate your acetylcholine, dopamine, and other neurotransmitters and will give your brain a moderate yet consistent source of energy. This is very important, because according to studies, paying attention, self-control, dealing with stress, decision-making, and performing cognitive tasks can deplete the energy source of your brain and make it harder for you to stay motivated and maintain your drive.

You should also eliminate processed foods and gluten from your diet. Gluten is not ideal for your body because it is difficult to digest. It causes an inflammatory response that goes directly to your brain. If you eat gluten, your brain will suffer inflammation because a type of plaque interferes with the proper communication between your brain cells.

Make sure you also increase your intake of foods that are rich in omega-3, such as fish oil. Omega-3 can help improve your brain function because it enables quick connections to be made by the chemical messengers in your brain.

In addition, try drinking energy drinks. According to The British Psychology Society, consuming energy drinks can increase your self-control by providing your body with glucose. If you do not like energy drinks, you can just gargle them. It is alright to not swallow them, because swirling a drink that contains glucose can give your glucose levels a boost.

Conclusion

Thank you again for purchasing this book!

I hope this book helped you learn ways to increase your self-control and willpower.

The next step is to apply what you have learned from this book.

Thank you and good luck!

www.ingramcontent.com/pod-product-compliance
Lightning Source LLC
Chambersburg PA
CBHW060444290526
45793CB00002B/570